8 SURPRISES AND STORIES BY JESUS

BRONWYN SHORT/BEVERLEY BIOSSERY

Aquila Press
PO Box A287, Sydney South 1235
Australia

www.youthworks.net
www.publications.youthworks.net
email: sales@youthworks.net
Ph: (612) 8268 3344
Fax: (612) 8268 3357

Copyright © 2007 Bronwyn Short and Beverley Boissery

All rights reserved. No part of this publication may be reproduced, stored in a retrieval system, or transmitted in any form or by any means, electronic, mechanical, photocopying, recording, or otherwise (except for brief passages for purposes of review) without the prior permission of Aquila Press.

Scripture taken from The Holy Bible, New International Version. Copyright ©1973, 1978, and 1984 by International Bible Society. 'NIV' and 'New International Version' are trademarks registered in the United States Patent and Trademark office by International Bible Society.

NATIONAL LIBRARY OF AUSTRALIA
ISBN 978 192 1137792

Cover design Joy Lankshear

CONTENTS

1. Jesus startles his disciples — 7
2. Fatted calf tastes great — 12
3. Jesus stirs up the establishment — 18
4. Jesus shocks a grieving woman — 24
5. Jesus surprises a doubter — 31
6. A shattering diagnosis — 37
7. Very sour grapes — 43
8. Shaky real estate — 50

HOW TO GET THE MOST OUT OF THESE STUDIES

1 Do each study before you meet as a group to work through it.

2 Ask God to help you understand what you read. If you are new to prayer, you might like to say the following:

God, help me understand what I read. Help me understand what it tells about you and your son, Jesus. Help me to take the message in these words into my heart so that they result in a vital and living relationship with you. Amen

3 Use a modern translation. We usually quote from the New International Version of the Bible, so that might be a good translation to use.

4 Find a quiet spot with as few distractions as possible.

5 Turn off your mobile phone.

6 Don't worry if you can't find an answer to a question—mark it and go on to the next one. Remember to ask about it in your group session.

SUMMARIES AND OUTLINES

For some of you, question 1 of each study will seem off-putting. You will think, 'I haven't had to do this since school.' Others may say, 'I've never been taught this. I don't know how to do it. I'm going on to the next question'.

Question 1 is emphasised for several very good reasons. Summarising makes you read the whole passage and that gives you a better understanding when you tackle the questions. It's like reading a book through before doing detailed work on it. It helps comprehension.

But there are far more important reasons for question 1 than these. Reading, praying and asking for God's guidance are the keys to being open to God talking to you directly. It's your one-on-one time with God with no one else interrupting or intervening. Reading, thinking and summarising are the keys to independent Bible study.

So, how do you do it? Here's two approaches which may help.

APPROACH #1 – LOOK FOR THE CENTRAL PERSON IN THE STORY

Then ask:

1. Who is being talked about?
   HINT: In all of these studies, it's Jesus.
2. What is he/she/it doing or teaching?

Essential point: What is the importance of that action?

APPROACH #2 – FOR USE WHEN THE PASSAGE DEALS WITH CONCEPTS, IDEAS OR TEACHINGS

1. What is the overall topic?
2. What are the main things written about it?

Essential point: What is the implication of those things?

1 MARK 4:35–41
JESUS STARTLES HIS DISCIPLES

As this is the first study, take time as a group to go through the suggested procedures. Read the pages on summarising and the rationale for it. Then pray the following:

God, help me understand what I read. Help me understand what it tells about you and your son, Jesus. Help me to take the message in these words into my heart so that they result in a vital and living relationship with you. Amen

1 Read the passage. Think about it. Now, write a 3–5 point summary of it.

-
-
-
-
-

What is the main point of the passage? What does it teach about Jesus?

2 What details are clues that an eyewitness gave Mark the facts about the story?

3 How did the disciples react throughout the story? Identify their emotions.

4 What did they accuse Jesus of in verse 38? What do you think they meant by it?

5 Look at the question in verse 41: 'Who is this man?'
What do you think the disciples must have understood about Jesus before the storm happened?

6 From this passage, how would you answer the disciples' question?

7 The author, Mark, only mentions the disciples were 'terrified' after the storm had subsided and the waves had been calmed. Why might they have been this afraid when they were in no physical danger?

8 What do you think Mark, wants us to understand from this story?

9 Go back to question 1. Did your understanding of the main point change as you worked through the passage? If so, revise it now.

QUESTIONS?

NOTES

If we look at the beginning of the chapter, we see that Jesus has been teaching about who he is and why he came to earth. He did this by telling stories, or parables (verse 33) to whomever would listen—be it one person or thousands. After teaching publicly, Jesus took the time and trouble to further explain these stories to his closest followers, the disciples (verse 34). Obviously, judging from this study, they, like the crowds, rarely understood the point of the stories.

In a way, it is such an encouragement to us that the disciples, the men who ate, drank, walked and lived with Jesus, had as much trouble understanding who he was as we do. Time after time in the New Testament, we read of Jesus asking in near frustration, 'Don't you understand yet?'

This particular event is a transition. The disciples still haven't worked out who Jesus is. Instead of telling stories, Jesus interacts with four different natural elements that govern human life to reveal his power over them: nature (as in this study); evil (Mark 5:1–20); chronic illness (5:25–34); and death (5:21–24 and 5:35–43).

The author, Mark, beautifully sets his account up as an historical incident. He gives details that can only come from an eyewitness—the cushion, the other boats, etc. It's as if he's saying, 'This really happened. You can believe it.' Thus, we're directed to not only the storm but its consequences.

Even today, sudden windstorms happen frequently on the Sea of Galilee. Mountains surround the sea except in the south where the Jordan River flows towards the Dead Sea. Thus, the sea is susceptible to the effects of Mediterranean winds from the south which whip into the box canyon and wreak havoc. A storm, such as the one Jesus quelled, would provoke violent wave action, hence the double-barrel nature of the miracle.

Mark was not only a good writer but a clever historian. He expected this story to make his readers think as they, like the disciples, begin to answer the crucial question in verse 41: 'Who is this man?' Unfortunately, as the rest of his gospel shows, the disciples took a long time to work out the answer to the question. Jesus died knowing they still hadn't got it. In fact, it was only after his death, burial and resurrection that they, like us, completely believed in Jesus through faith. And, like them, all of us must answer the question: 'Who is this man?'

2

LUKE 15:11–32

FATTED CALF TASTES GREAT

1 Pray for guidance. Read the passage, think about it, then write a 3–5 point summary of it.

- younger son – Willfulness, selfishness reckless asking forgiveness
- Causing the father great unhappiness but giving his son forgiveness celebrates
-
- Older son
-

What is the main point of the passage? "Love Conquers All"
What does it teach about God or Jesus?
God is patient + loving – God wants us to repent
God is willing to forgive + come to him
God's love is constant, patient
God is just merciful + kind

She dying — She cosay.
"Lost + Found" Lost is Found"

2 Give the story an alternative title. Or, write a headline for it.
God is Always Forgiving!!
Love acceptance + forgiveness

3 Make three quick character sketches of the story's protagonists (main characters):
a) the father — full of love, mercy, forgiving, hardworking

b) the younger son — repenting, asking forgiveness, adulterous, reckless, spoiled, immature

c) the older son — self righteous, bitter, jealous, angry, resentful, sense of duty.

Which one do you relate to? Why? — Surprise
Father — I would have forgiven the younger son.

4 Trace (or graph) the path of the younger son's journey, both downward and homeward.
humility

~~fatted calf. any reference to the fatted calf~~

5 What strikes you most about the father's behaviour towards his two sons?

Loving. Hope. Watching
Forgiving — Respected his son's freedoms/opinions
Patient   Didn't take away the existing consequences
Rejoiced
Willing to listen

6 This story is part of a group of three stories dealing with God's reaction to lost property. Read Luke 15:1–7. ✓
What is the shepherd's reaction when he finds his lost sheep?

Rejoicing w/ friends over the one

Continue reading (verses 8–10). ✓
What is the woman's reaction when she finds her lost coin?

Joy —

7 What is the father's reaction when his son returns home? Is it similar or dissimilar to the other two stories?

Joy & Celebration

8 What do these three stories teach about God and his reactions when we stop being lost? Does this change the way you think about God?

Mercy –
Joyful in finding the lost –
When we are lost – God does not give up
We matter to God!
all God Loves Everyone!

9 If you are still 'lost,' what is stopping you from turning, or returning to God? Nothing! Side tracked off

Pride | Want
Shame | keep
Given up | you
from returning!

10 Go back to question 1 and your answer for the main point of the story. Has working with the passage changed your original idea? If so, what do you now see as the main point of the story?

No change
Love Forgiveness

Pharisees – like the older brother — filled with rebuke
Jews – younger brothers

QUESTIONS?

NOTES

It's always important to see passages in the Bible in their contexts, as questions 6 and 7 show. Otherwise, the original meaning can be frequently distorted or altered. To use an example from secular literature, most people know the following quote from Shakespeare's Romeo and Juliet: 'Romeo, Romeo, wherefore art thou Romeo?' Few, however, know the context and therefore, the meaning of Juliet's question is lost or greatly obscured.

In much the same way, most people know about the prodigal son. The father and older brother's reactions are less well known. Moreover, we've usually read the story through human-centric eyes and identify with either the younger or older son. Luke, however, has given a clue as to how we should read the story by placing it in a group of three about lost property.

The common element in the three stories is the reaction of the finder. JOY. It's hard for us to believe, isn't it, that God the Father would rejoice when we turn to him through faith in Jesus. Like the lost son, when we:

* admit our mistakes (sins);

* are sorry for them;

* acknowledge that the penalty imposed by God on our sins is death;

* and accept that only by the death and resurrection of Jesus could that penalty be paid and our slate wiped clean by God.

God rejoices! In church language, the above process is called confession, repentance, and acceptance of our salvation. However worded, the message is unambiguous and clear. When we confess our sins and acknowledge that Jesus paid the penalty for them, we are saved from their consequences. God rejoices because we are 'found.' More than that, his joy is meant to be shared, as the fatted calf analogy shows.

It is so easy to see that the younger son needed to repent and return to his father that we frequently miss the lesson to be learned from the older son. As his story shows us, staying at 'home', doesn't prevent rebellion. We can go to church all our lives, for example, yet be as distant from our Father (God), as lost as the younger son when he rebelled. In the parable, both sons needed the Father's forgiveness but only one clearly understood that necessity.

Jesus often taught these short stories called parables. One reason may have been that all of us love stories. We all love puzzles, as well. The parables are often enigmatic, yet they reveal so much about Jesus and why he came to live amongst us. At first glance, they often seem simple. Yet, once we begin to think about them, we're often overwhelmed by their complexity and the teaching Jesus managed to pack into these stories.

The parable of the prodigal son is a classic 'win-win' story. Being found means joy for God and joy for us. It makes being 'lost' pointless, doesn't it?

3

MARK 2:13–22

JESUS STIRS UP THE ESTABLISHMENT

1 Pray, then read the passage. Think, then summarise it in 3–5 points.

-

-

-

-

-

What is the story's main point? What does it teach about Jesus?

2 Why do you think Mark tells us this story?
What is so striking about this action of Jesus?

3 Try to imagine Levi's emotions. What are they?
There are clues in the passage.

4 Why are the religious teachers so appalled?

5 Jesus' reply is very revealing.
Why has he come and what do you think he means by his reply?

6 What sparks the next controversy?
How does Jesus reveal even more about himself and who he is?

7 Follow the use of the words 'old' and 'new' in verses 21–22. What do you understand from their use in this passage?

8 How is the 'call' of Levi related to the last part of the story?

9 It is often said that Christianity is not a religion but a relationship. What do you think?

10 How does this story help someone who thinks they are 'not the religious type' or are 'too far gone' to answer the call of Jesus?

Revisit question 1. Did your main point hold up? If not, revise it now.

QUESTIONS?

NOTES

Jesus met Levi near the important town of Capernaum in western Galilee. Capernaum, situated in a fertile agricultural plain, had about 15,000 inhabitants at the time and most people worked in the well-established fish catching and preserving industries. The town was so close to the tetrarchy of Herod Antipas that a large number of Roman soldiers and royal officials lived in the town and added to its wealth and importance.

More importantly, for the context of the passage, people travelling through the area had to pay tolls. The collectors, men like Levi, were widely loathed and despised and, to us, this attitude is initially hard to understand. After all, while we don't like paying taxes, we accept those who work in the various revenue branches of government as law-abiding civil servants. Not so in the days of Jesus! Maybe the best modern comparison to Levi and his ilk would be our reactions to the Hell's Angels. Fear and loathing.

Levi and his colleagues were a law unto themselves. While there was a set rate for the tolls, these biblical 'tax collectors' extorted whatever sums they could from those travelling the roads. They would never be used as witnesses in legal cases because their testimony would not be believed. Their reputation was such that they were banned from being judges. Respectable people did not willingly associate with them and would never go to their houses for dinner.

These factors make the actions of Jesus, therefore, truly astounding. Jesus just didn't go to Levi's house for a meal. He had previously asked Levi to be his student or disciple. This request in itself shocked the law-obsessed Pharisees. In their world, students applied to study under them and they accepted only the best of the best. They would never have dreamed of soliciting any students, much less someone as notorious as Levi.

Jesus chooses this incident to define his mission. He hasn't left heaven and come to earth to serve the cream of the crop. As he says in verse 17, he has come for the 'sick,' the sinners. God's kingdom isn't for the righteous, for those like the Pharisees who prize their good deeds. Rather, God's kingdom is for everyone, even society's outcasts. That afternoon in Capernaum so long ago, gives life and hope today. Few of us can boast, as the Pharisees did, of our righteousness. We look in the mirror far too often to make that claim! As Jesus said, he came to bring sinners, like Levi, like us, into the kingdom of God. His invitation to follow him wasn't just a one-off to Levi. It's open to us today.

How do we react? Do we pretend, like the Pharisees, that we have no need for Jesus in our life? Levi offers a model to show how we should respond. He immediately accepted Jesus' offer, left his lucrative job and went with Jesus. We know he is overjoyed about this change of lifestyle because he hosted a lavish banquet that very night to share that joy with his co-workers and friends. He was grateful and wanted everyone to meet his new leader.

Strangely, many of us today might say we've never heard of Levi. Yet, we have, because he is better known by his other name, Matthew. It's amazing to connect Levi and the first gospel, isn't it? It seems strange that the incident in Capernaum should have had such far-reaching effects. Strange, of course, only for those of us who don't know the transforming work of Jesus. But it is amazing. We don't know the name of the most important official in Capernaum or who was the richest person in the town. Yet the name of the notorious tax collector, the man who was so despised by his fellow citizens that he couldn't be a judge, has been revered for centuries because of his testimony about Jesus.

Today, in the twenty-first century, Matthew/Levi continues to share his knowledge of Jesus and Jesus continues to say to all of us, 'Follow me.' How we respond is as big a choice for us as it was for people in ancient Capernaum. Are we like the Pharisees? Does our belief in our own goodness, in technical prowess, or in the latest spiritual discovery blind us to our need of Jesus? Are we so arrogant and proud that we believe we don't have to repent? Or, are we like Levi? Do we hear the call of Jesus and immediately change our lives?

Now, as it was then, the choice is ours.

4 JOHN 20:1–18
JESUS SHOCKS A GRIEVING WOMAN

This story, and that of the crucifixion of Jesus, are so well-known that it's impossible to read or hear about them without feeling a bit blasé. Yet, try to imagine that you live in the first century A.D. A scroll of John's gospel has come to your town. Someone reads it and, as you listen to the story of Jesus, you become entranced. What a wonderful man! you think. So compassionate. So compelling. And, so wise. You cry when the story of his death is read and feel a myriad emotions—grief, anger that he should have been treated so badly, sadness because such a good man has left this earth and outrage because his friends, the disciples, disgraced themselves so badly. You think it's the end of the story. Wait, the reader tells you, there's more.

Try very hard to imagine what you might have felt as you heard about Mary and the disciples on the morning of the third day. You probably sat forward, on the edge of your seat, wondering what will happen next.

1 Remember that feeling as you pray and then read this passage. Think, then write a 3–5 point summary of it or your own response to it.

- Sadness for Mary @ her loss of Jesus
- Resurrection ?
-

EIGHT SURPRISES AND STORIES BY JESUS

-
-

What is the main point of the story? What does it teach about Jesus?

& changed our relationship c God

Jesus resurrection is the key to the Christian faith this is confirmed

Jesus overcame death — after such torture — he must of been "the Son of God". accepting Jesus as God our Father —

2 Put yourself in Mary's place that tragic morning. What is running through your mind?

Compassion for her — she would be in shock *torment* she certainly ~~did not~~ expect to see him — overcome w grief.

Nicodemus + Joseph

3 What did Mary intend doing at the tomb of Jesus? For some insight see Luke 24:1.

Anointing the body of Jesus. To see Jesus one last time — showing her love r respect through her grief.

JESUS SHOCKS A GRIEVING WOMAN

4 How do we know from the passage that a resurrection was the last thing on the mind of Mary (and Peter and John)?

Surprised that Jesus was not in the tomb, only considered that he had been taken - went back to their homes - shocked, sad, confused -

5 What can we deduce from the evidence of the grave clothes? What do they tell us about whether or not the body was stolen?

20.9 the grave clothes were left as if Jesus body had simply vacated them, passed right through them. The linens looked as if they were shaped around his body - undisturbed.

6 Why do you think Mary and the others failed to believe what Jesus had told them many times (e.g. in Mark 9:31) before he died? See verse 9 for help.

After they saw the empty tomb - only then did they remember what the scriptures and Jesus had said that he would die, but then he would also rise again. Betrayed, killed, John. He had risen, which he ahad he told them.

7 What do you think John, the author, meant when he wrote that the Scripture said, 'Jesus had to rise from the dead?' In other words, why did Jesus rise from the dead?

John 20.9 - Otherwise "death would not be defeated" Just as he said - Accomplishing all that he has promised. Jesus bodily resurrection shows us that the living Christ and not a false prophet or imposter is the ruler of God's Kingdom. We can be certain of our own resurrection because of Jesus Resurrection had to rise to fulfill prophecy.

8 How could Mary have mistaken Jesus for a gardener?

She was not expecting to see him - and he did not address her by name to begin with - calling her "Woman" - then after asking him (thinking he was the gardener) J

9 What makes her realise that he's Jesus?

He called her by name
She knows his voice

10 What job does Jesus give Mary (verses 17-18)?

Instructions to go to his disciples with the message that he was going to return to God the Father

11 In verse 17, Jesus says an astounding thing to Mary (after telling her not to cling to him). What is so amazing about what he tells her to say to the disciples? How has it been made possible?

- If he did not ascend to heaven - the Holy Spirit could not come

- Because of his death, resurrection + ascension (ascension) calls his disciples "brothers"

12 Go back and look at question 1. Do you need to revise your main point? If so, do it now.

QUESTIONS?

NOTES

When reading this passage, it is important to realise that John has crafted it so that readers cannot doubt his story of the resurrection. He chose his witnesses carefully. They were influential people whom the early Christians knew and respected. He gave the same care to the evidentiary detail.

Dan Brown's blockbuster, *The Da Vinci Code*, has once again made Mary Magdalene notorious. For hundreds of centuries she had been maligned as a prostitute, an error Pope Gregory endorsed in 591 A.D. The historical Mary came from Magdala, a town in Galilee. She seems to have been relatively affluent and was part of a group of influential women who supported Jesus and the disciples during their years of ministry. As the early Christian communities had great respect for her, it is not surprising that John selected her specifically as one of his witnesses to the resurrection of Jesus.

At dawn, on the third day after the crucifixion, Mary and the other women from Galilee went to the tomb with spices to anoint the body of Jesus. Maybe they didn't know that Nicodemus and Joseph had bravely carried out that task; maybe they simply wanted to make sure it had been done properly. Certainly, they wanted to show their love and respect for Jesus one last time. To their astonishment they saw that the stone blocking the entrance had been moved and (presumably, after looking in) saw that the tomb was empty. Immediately Mary ran off to tell Peter and John.

It is impossible to over-estimate the shock the disciples must have been in. Their best friend, their leader, the man they had devoted the last three years of their life to, had been crucified—one of the most shameful deaths in their world. By and large when the moment of crisis came, they had failed the test. Peter had denied knowing Jesus and the others, apart from John, seem to have deserted their dying leader. Once Jesus was dead, they holed up in Jerusalem until Mary's news galvanised Peter and John into action.

After running to the tomb, John stopped and looked in. The detail that etched itself into his memory was not that the stone had been moved. His first impression was the strips of linen and the cloth, which had been wrapped around the body, lying on the stone tomb. Later, when he followed Peter and entered the tomb, he noticed that the linen and cloth lay apart from each other.

So what, you might ask, is so important about these details?

That something happened to the body of Jesus, after it had been put into its tomb, is one of the best documented facts from the ancient world. It is beyond doubt that, when Mary, Peter and John went to the tomb, it was empty. The question has always been: what happened to the body? Did the Pharisees organise its removal? Did the Roman soldiers, who had been set to guard against the disciples removing the body, desert their posts and take the body away with them? Was the grave robbed? It is inconceivable that the body would be unwrapped in any of those scenarios, hence John's careful detailing of that fact.

John points out that Mary was the first person to see and hear the newly risen Jesus. She, not the male disciples, was commissioned to tell others of this amazing fact. No doubt she also told them that Jesus had somehow changed. She hadn't been allowed to touch him, as she presumably was used to doing, because Jesus was in the process of resuming his life with his Father. Their relationship had changed profoundly. No longer would it be an earthly friendship because, from now on, Jesus was her exalted king who would shortly sit at God's right hand.

During the last supper, Jesus had prepared his disciples for the future. No longer, for example, would he pray for them. Instead, they will pray directly to the Father using his name (John 16:23–26). This new reality is reiterated in verse 17 of this passage. Jesus was in transition. He was returning to his Father and their Father, to his God and their God. Through his death and resurrection, he transformed their relationship with God. Like Jesus, they too could call God 'Father'. No longer would those who believed in God need human intermediaries, such as priests. Jesus alone would be totally sufficient.

John wrote a carefully crafted gospel that culminates in this point. The humiliating death of Jesus is not the end of the story. Rather, it is the beginning of God's new reality in which all of us who accept Jesus discover the joy of calling God our Father. No matter how long we live or how much we study, the full implications of this encounter remain joyfully amazing.

5 JESUS SURPRISES A DOUBTER.

JOHN 20: 19–31

Thurs April

1 Pray for guidance. Read the passage, think about it, then write a 3–5 point summary of it.

- Jesus appears to his disciples, behind locked doors, scared of the Jews
- Thomas was not present @ that 1st meeting
- Stating that unless he had physical proof he would not be believing that this was
- actually "the Lord", who had appeared 8 days later
- Once Thomas had seen the physical evidence, he believed and stated "My Lord + My God!"
- "Then they were overjoyed!"
- Many other signs are performed.

What is the main point of the story? What does it teach about Jesus?

Blessed are those who have not ~~believed~~ seen and yet still believed [can have eternal life.]

- Jesus wanted to be believed and that he is the Christ, the son of God, and that by believing you may have life in his name.

Book of John — 12 chapters — Many signs — This was the greatest — culmination of signs

2. What further clues are given in this passage that the disciples were really not expecting the resurrection of Jesus?

overjoyed
- if they had been expecting Jesus - Thomas might have been there.
- Providing proof -

3. Why would Jesus show them his hands and side?

To give them physical proof that he was that same person who had been crucified + tortured.
Came into a locked room -
These disciples were the main original ones to spread the word →

4. What job does he give the disciples? What does he give them to help them do that task?

affirmation Spread the word -

5. How would you describe Thomas and his issues? Wanted proof!
What do they look like in today's world?

non-believer - without facts
Skeptical -

EIGHT SURPRISES AND STORIES BY JESUS

Acts - appeared to 500 people @ once following the resurrection.

6 How does Jesus show his mercy when dealing with Thomas?

- He doesn't further question him
- He continues to show him
- ★ i.e. by entering a locked room and continues to challenge him by his the conditions he has put on his belief.

7 Jesus doesn't challenge Thomas after he says he believes. What is so remarkable about that?

Jesus is trusting that there will be belief now on the part of Thomas now that he has seen — ! nothing further is required!

Jesus previously said not ye of little faith

8 This passage gives great encouragement for those who, like us, weren't there to see the risen Christ. What is it?

Faith — to believe
No proof (other) required — the scriptures are what we have —

9 Rather than that visual sighting of Jesus, where does John tell us to place our faith (verses 30–31)?

By Jesus performed many other miraculous signs in the disciples presence
By believing you will have life in his name!
Everlasting life
The testimonies are to help us!
of the ancient believers

10 What does he want us to understand and believe from all he has written?

that he is faithworthy and speaks with the authority of God

Jesus is the Christ, Son of God

Believe?
Obey
Follow } Holy Spirit was sent by God.

11 What is promised to us when we do understand and believe?

That we will have ever lasting life

Being saved and walking in that salvation

What, if anything, is keeping you from believing that Jesus is Christ, the Son of God?

No!

12 Go back to question 1. Review your original key idea. If you need to revise it, do it now.

QUESTIONS?

NOTES

Mary's story is unique. Thomas' story is far more mundane. So ordinary, in fact, that all of us can see ourselves in his, 'I won't believe until you give me proof'.

- <u>Although all God asks of us is faith</u>, we frequently <u>demand</u> concrete evidence before giving it. In this passage, Thomas <u>doesn't believe the evidence of his ten best associates.</u> Moreover, for three years he had travelled Palestine with them, listening to the teaching of Jesus and seeing the miracles for himself. According to Mark's gospel (Chapter 6, verses 7–13), <u>Jesus had given him and the others power to heal and drive out demons</u>. When the Pharisees requested concrete evidence of a miracle (John 4:48), Thomas would have heard the scornful reply of Jesus.

In this passage, Thomas proves that he hasn't understood much of Jesus' teaching. His response to his fellow disciples' report of the risen Jesus is as far away from faith as is possible. He even put parameters around belief. 'I will believe,' he says in verse 25, 'when I see the scars of the nails in his hands and put my fingers where the nails were and my hand in his side (i.e. in the spear wound)'.

In response, Jesus yet once more demonstrates his understanding and grace. He appears again to the disciples at a time when Thomas is amongst them. To help them further understand the supernatural nature of his risen body, he enters a locked room to begin the dramatic dialogue of verses 27–29. He systematically challenges the conditions Thomas put on belief until Thomas affirms that Jesus is his Lord and God. Jesus does not reject this stupendous affirmation which, as John teaches in verse 31 of the passage, is the pivotal declaration for our eternal life.

It is almost impossible to find words to describe the exciting significance of this declaration. The way people get to know truth and find eternal life has shifted profoundly. Up until the resurrection, eternal life came by hearing and 'seeing' Jesus and his works in the flesh. The resurrection created a vitally new and equally trustworthy way for everyone to know Christ. As John writes in verse 31, 'these things are written [so] that you may believe that Jesus is the Christ, the Son of God and that by believing you may have life in his name.' Faith in Christ now comes by reading and believing the written account we find in the Bible. This is incredibly good news for everyone, including us, who live after the time Christ actually lived on earth. Jesus himself says that our faith is 'blessed'. We don't need to sentimentally wonder what it might have been like to have been in Palestine about 30 A.D.

Jesus is absolutely 'faithworthy' and he speaks with the authority of God on this subject. He assures us that we can be certain of the truth of his claims and be as intimate with him as the disciples were if we read his words, believe them and thus believe in him.

It really is that simple and, so, the challenge comes to each of us. We must all individually trust Christ and his claims and we do this on the basis of what we read in the Bible. Wonderfully, when we do, we receive the gift of eternal life from the living, resurrected source of life—Christ himself.

6

MARK 7:1–23
A SHATTERING DIAGNOSIS

1 Pray for guidance. Read the passage, think about it, then write a 3–5 point summary of it.

-
-
-
-
-

What is the main point of the story? What does it teach about Jesus?

2 Who are the protagonists (main characters)?

3 What verses make it obvious that Mark is writing for non-Jewish readers?

4 Why do you think Mark tells this very Jewish story to his non-Jewish audience? What verses did you base your answer on?

5 What is the Pharisees' criticism of Jesus?
(See the notes for an explanation of them.)

6 Why do you think Jesus would quote the Old Testament (verses 6–7) as part of his answer?

7 Using the following verses, what does Jesus perceive the problem or danger of the rules of the Pharisees to be?

Verse 7

Verse 8

Verse 9

Verse 13

8 What does Jesus diagnose as the real problem for all of us?

9 According to Jesus, why doesn't religious activity and/or rules solve our real spiritual problems?

10 Give an example from your own life, your church or community that Jesus could use to prove his diagnosis.

QUESTIONS?

NOTES

When Jesus lived, the religious leaders of his Jewish world were the Sadducees and the Pharisees. The Sadducees were relatively small in number and notable for their disbelief in resurrection. The Pharisees, on the other hand, did believe in an afterlife and their self-given mission was to ensure the salvation of their fellow Jews. They not only taught the more than 600 rules found in Exodus, Numbers and Leviticus of the Old Testament, but enlarged upon them, adding sections and subsections, made rules from traditions, and tried to make everyone live by this rigid code.

They believed that everyone would be saved from the judgment of God if they kept all the rules. This is one reason they challenged Jesus whenever they saw his disciples breaking the rules or whenever he did himself, as in Mark 2:23–24, for example, when his disciples picked a few heads of grain on the Sabbath, defying one rule which dictated that no work could be done during it. By and large, Jesus condemned them strongly, comparing them to 'whitewashed tombs,' (Matthew 23:27) meaning that their hypocrisy masked spiritual decay.

In retrospect, it is so easy to see their mistake. History proves, time and time again, that it is impossible for society to keep its own rules, much less the rules of God. Although we have this proof, we are still, unfortunately, Pharisaical in our religious beliefs and rules. If we go to church on Sunday, we'll be all right, we tell ourselves. Or, we might sacrifice something, like chocolate during Lent, to appease God. Some of us tell ourselves that if we read the Bible through every year, we'll be okay. Others equate sin with crime and say, because I haven't been charged with anything, I don't sin.

Keeping rules and doing the right thing cannot solve our basic problem. They're bandaids and, as such, cannot change our hearts. The problem is far more deep-seated. As the next study will show, our basic fault is rebellion against God. Therefore, although it is vastly unfashionable to say it, we sin and we do it in the traditional ways—thoughts, words and deeds. As sinners, we cannot make ourselves righteous. Think about it. If we could, why would God have let his dearly loved son go through the agony of the crucifixion?

This, ultimately, is why Jesus and the Pharisees were at such loggerheads. He taught that he was the only way to God and that all that was needed was to believe in him. Through his death, descent into hell and resurrection, he paid the price for us, he brokered our realignment with God. When God looks upon us then, he sees us through the lens of his son and accepts us.

It doesn't matter how many rules we keep, if we don't accept the salvation offered by Jesus, God won't accept us.

7

MARK 11:27–12:12

VERY SOUR GRAPES

1 Pray for guidance. Read the passage, think about it, then write a 3–5 point summary of it.

-
-
-
-
-

What is the main point of the passage? What does it teach about Jesus?

2 What questions do the chief priests, the teachers of the law, and the elders ask Jesus?

3 How does Jesus answer them in verses 29–33?

4 In the following parable, or story, who is Jesus really identifying as:

a) the vineyard owner?

b) the tenant farmers?

c) the servants sent by the owner?

d) the son?

5 How is it clear from the story that the son is special? See verses 6–8 particularly.

6 What was the real reason for the tenants' rebellion?

7 What does Jesus teach, therefore, about our rejection of God and his son?

8 What does this parable teach about the core of sin?

9 According to this parable, what's wrong with saying, 'I believe in God but I don't really believe in Jesus'?

10 What do verses 9–11 reveal about God's response to rebellion and rejection of his son?

11 Go back to question 3. What is the real answer Jesus gave to those questions asked by the religious insiders? What does this answer teach us about who he is and how we need to respond to him?

QUESTIONS?

NOTES

This study is probably the most important one in *Eight Surprises and Stories* because in it Jesus explains exactly who he is and why he came to earth.

They say that location is everything but, in this situation, timing is crucial for Jesus had less than one week left on earth to help people understand who he was and why he had left heaven. Less than one week to convince people of their rebellion and the need to accept him as the landlord's son.

A short time before this confrontation with the religious elite of Jerusalem, he had entered the city on a donkey. People had waved palm fronds and shouted their happiness (see Mark 11:9). Not surprisingly, the religious leaders were outraged and demanded Jesus show them his credentials. Jesus first replied with an unanswerable question, then told this story which appears simple—at first glance.

The story revolves around an absentee landlord who planted and equipped a vineyard. When he rented it out to tenants, they refused to pay the rent. He sent emissaries, servants or agents to collect it. The tenants abused all of them—beating some, killing others. Finally, the owner played his trump card. He sent his dearly loved son thinking, erroneously, that the tenants would have to respect his heir.

By telling this story, Jesus really answered the questions of the religious elite asked in 11:28. In his parable, he quoted Psalm 118, verses 22–23, obviously referring to himself as the stone being rejected by them. But there was another allusion which probably ran through their minds as they listened to this not-so-simple story. They must have thought of words written by the prophet Isaiah, 700 years earlier, who, in Isaiah 5, verses 1–7, spoke of a vineyard which yielded only the bad grapes of bloodshed and distress instead of justice and righteousness. Isaiah is explicit and interprets his story in verse 7. The owner of the vineyard is the Lord God Almighty. The vineyard is Israel. As God asks in 5:1–4, what more could he have done? He had created it, protected it and planted only the best vines. Why then did it continue to produce bad grapes? The only solution was its destruction. Similarly, Jesus warned, the owner of the vineyard will react when his son is killed. He will destroy the tenants and give the vineyard to others who will obey and respect him.

The men who listened to the story must have identified other key elements in it. When Jesus answered their demand for credentials, he referred to John the Baptist, a prophet who had explicitly identified him as the messiah, the man who would be the world's saviour. The leaders had paid no attention to this endorsement, just as the tenants had paid no attention to the agents sent by the vineyard's owner. If they were astute, they must have understood this subtle condemnation. Instead of repenting though, their resolution to arrest and eliminate Jesus became greater than ever and, within the week, they would watch him die. Only God knows if any of them thought back to that last attempt by Jesus to teach them.

As usual, though, Jesus' story speaks throughout the ages. All of us must ask and answer the questions in it. Our world is the vineyard and we live in it at God's pleasure. Do we pay our rents? Or, do we, like the tenants in this story, rebel against God and refuse? Do we reject his agents who try to tell us about him? If so, we must take the warning in the story seriously. After all, what more can God do for us than give his son to reconcile us to him? And, as well, God's resolution to punish those who kill his son must never be underestimated. Killing Jesus doesn't just mean the crucifixion of two thousand years ago. It means trivialising him, ignoring him, replacing him with the gods of our own choosing.

Unless Jesus is front and centre in our lives, we have much to fear. God's love for his son is far greater than any human parent's love. His anguish when Jesus was killed was correspondingly greater. God has done his part. He has given us a fully equipped world to enjoy. He has given us the ability to choose. Do we give God his due and produce righteousness and justice? Do we listen to his agents who tell us about him? Do we reject his son?

We can live, as Isaiah puts it, in 'the garden of God's delight' or we can, like the religious men in this story, ignore the claims of God and try to eliminate Jesus from our world. The choice is that stark and that simple.

8

MATTHEW 7:13–29

SHAKY REAL ESTATE

1 Pray for guidance. Read the passage, think about it, then write a 3–5 point summary of it.

-
-
-
-
-

What is the main point of the passage? What is Jesus saying?

Following Jesus will always have its challenges as intended. Your goal will be very specific as to do following Jesus & pleasing God, making independent choices towards achieving the reward of being welcomed into the kingdom of God

2 Reread verses 13–14. How does Jesus describe the two:

	GATES	ROADS	DESTINATIONS
a)	Narrow small	lonley difficult	leads to life to enter heaven
b)	undefined wide	popular easy broad	perdition prey to false prophets untruths destruction

3 Why is it so hard to follow Jesus and so easy not to?

Hard to follow — Few do it
- singular goal - heaven
- unpopular
- hindrances
- personal struggling
- distractions

very persuasive

4 Why does Jesus think false prophets are so dangerous? How can we identify them?

- Give advice → leads to destruction
- Point people in the wrong direction
- Self serving
- Deceives people
- Do they lead people closer to God

SHAKY REAL ESTATE

5 Basing your answer on verses 21–23, what response is Jesus looking for from those listening to him?

the truth
A personal relationship with Christ
acceptance of him as the Saviour
and our obedience to him
Put his teachings into practise

6 What does it mean to 'do the will of my Father'?

Live and act as God wants us to!

7 How do verses 24–27 shed light on doing God's will?

Putting the words of Jesus into practise/

Knowing Gods word

8 In the illustration Jesus uses in verses 24–27, what do you think the storm means? Remember to think about it in its context—i.e. the preceding verses.

Trials & tribulations

EIGHT SURPRISES AND STORIES BY JESUS

9. What are the differences between the two houses in this story?

A House with a Solid Foundation

A House with No Foundation is likened to a foolish man who doesn't listen to Jesus after he has spoken — will have no meaning to his life.

one is protection by weather   ignoring!

10. According to Jesus, what is wisdom and what is foolishness? What are most people's definitions of these words?

Wisdom
learned knowledge combined w/ life's experiences

Foolishness
using poor judgement inability to draw on lifes experiences

11. Why would Jesus conclude his sermon with this vivid picture?

To provide a dramatic example that hopefully be understood by the contrasting example presented!

12 Does this affect the way you listen to and respond to the words of Jesus? If not, why not?

Yes it does

QUESTIONS?

NOTES

The introduction to this passage comes in Matthew 4:23: 'Jesus went throughout Galilee, teaching in their synagogues, preaching the good news of the kingdom, and healing every disease and sickness among the people'. Naturally enough, news of this incredible man spread to Syria (immediately north of Galilee), the Decapolis to the east, and south to Jerusalem and Judea. Crowds swarmed to wherever Jesus went. One day, the mass of people was so large, Jesus climbed up on a mountainside, sat down and began to talk to them. This teaching is known as the Sermon on the Mount. Most people, if they have heard of it, know the very first part, the Beatitudes—a group of sayings which begin with 'Blessed are... .' Few know the rest of the sermon.

This passage is the most difficult of all those selected for study in this series. It is not based on an incident to give it human interest. Neither is the teaching wrapped up in a story. Instead, Jesus gives the hundreds gathered to hear him a terrible warning. After telling them about the road that leads to life, he warns that there will come a time of judgment. He will deny entrance to many seeking to enter heaven because, as he says in this sermon, 'I never knew you'. So, right from the beginning of his public life,

Jesus was concerned that those who came to see and hear him, not only heard what he had to say, but heeded and put into practice what he told them. To help them do this, he identifies various hindrances.

He speaks of two gates, two roads and two destinations. One of these roads is the no-brainer. It's the one almost everyone seems to take. It's easy, but Jesus warns that it leads to destruction. The other is lonelier. Few take it. Yet, as verse 14 tells us, it's 'the road that leads to life.' The concept of the road not taken is one that intrigues us. The poet Robert Frost wrote about it early in the twentieth century, concluding:

> 'and I – I took the one less travelled by
> And that has made all the difference'.

Jesus went further. The road through the narrow gate is the only one we can travel on if we want to enter heaven.

There are many who would persuade us differently. Jesus, who defined himself as the truth (John 14:6), calls these people false prophets. They might look as harmless and as attractive as sheep, yet they are ferocious wolves because their advice leads to destruction. Study them, he tells us. Don't accept them at face value, even if they make mention of Jesus. Analyse their results carefully. Only those who do God's will, those who walk on the narrow road, who accept that their path is not an easy one, will enter heaven.

Following Jesus is not easy. It has never been and was never intended to be. Following Jesus means that your path will be different from most people's broad road. Your ambition is different. Rather than building a fortune, or making yourself a celebrity, you will be seeking to please God. You will be building your life on the foundation of his word, no matter how unpopular it is. Your goals won't be short term, or even long term as most people today define it. Your goal is heaven. Your goal is meeting Jesus there and having him say, 'Well done' rather than 'I never knew you'.

And yet for all the hardship associated with the small gate and the narrow road, following Jesus also means a life of joy and love. Although few travel that road with us, we are never alone and never unloved. Heaven, and being welcomed into God's presence, is the almost unimaginable reward because travelling that road with Jesus is worth the price in itself. So, don't be deterred by its apparent unpopularity, by accounts of its hardship, or by false teachers.

To change metaphors, build your house upon the rock of Jesus so that when the storm of judgment comes, he says, 'Welcome to my Father's house'.

SHAKY REAL ESTATE